**SPECTRUM®**
**READERS**

LEVEL 2

P9-CBU-935

# LOOK CLOSELY!
# Hidden Animals

By Katharine Kenah

Carson-Dellosa
Publishing

An imprint of Carson-Dellosa Publishing, LLC
P.O. Box 35665
Greensboro, NC 27425-5665

carsondellosa.com

Printed in the USA. All rights reserved.
ISBN 978-1-62399-144-9

01-002131120

Some animals hide
to stay safe from enemies.
They change color.
They change shape.
They have spots.
They have stripes.

Turn the page to see how some
animals hide in the wild.

# Polar Bear

Look closely. What do you see?
You see a polar bear and its cub.
They live in a land of ice and snow.
White fur keeps them warm.
It also makes them hard to see.

# Stick Insect

Look closely. What do you see?
You see a stick insect.
A small head and a long,
thin body make it hard to see.
It looks like a tree branch.

# Gecko

Look closely. What do you see?
You see a gecko.
It uses its toes to climb trees.
Its brown, bumpy skin makes it
hard to see on a log.

# Bengal Tiger

Look closely. What do you see?
You see a Bengal tiger.
Each tiger has a different set of stripes.
The stripes make the tiger
hard to see in tall grass.

# Leafy Sea Dragon

Look closely. What do you see?
You see a leafy sea dragon.
Its skin grows flaps that look like
waving seaweed.
Hungry fish do not see
the leafy sea dragon.

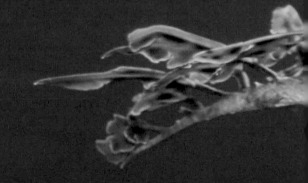

# Peacock Flounder

Look closely. What do you see?
You see a peacock flounder.
It lives in the sand and mud
under the sea.
Its skin changes color
to look like its home.

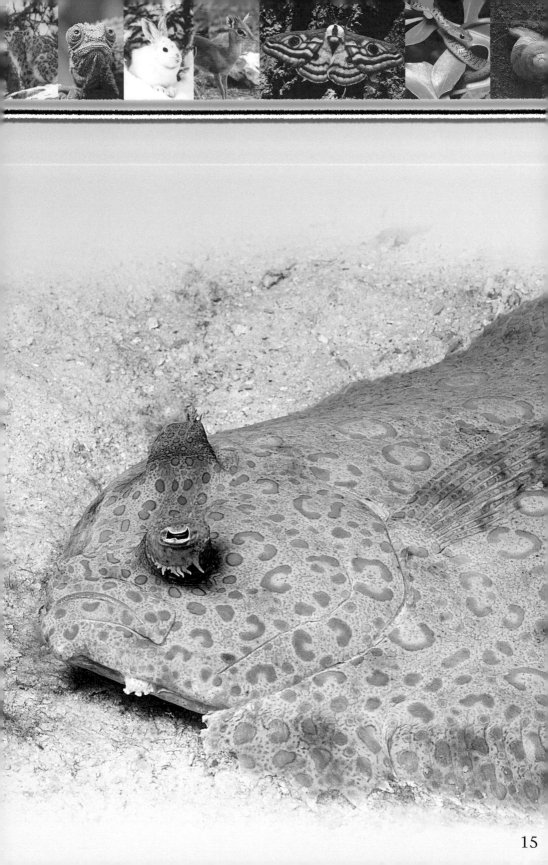

# Bullfrog

Look closely. What do you see?
You see a bullfrog.
Its dark stripes and yellow-green color
look like water and grass.
It hides well in a pond or stream.

# Snow Leopard

Look closely. What do you see?
You see a snow leopard.
It lives in high places with lots of snow.
Its pale fur and dark spots make it
hard to see among snow and rocks.

# Chameleon

Look closely. What do you see?
You see a chameleon.
It can be brown on the ground.
It can turn green in a tree.
A chameleon can change
its color quickly!

# Snowshoe Hare

Look closely. What do you see?
You see a snowshoe hare.
Its fur is brown in the summer
and white in the winter.
The hare's fur helps it hide
from other animals.

# Dik-Dik

Look closely. What do you see?
You see a dik-dik.
It is small and quick.
Its brown fur makes it
hard to see in the woods.

# Moth

Look closely. What do you see?
You see a moth.
Its wings are hard to see
next to the gray tree bark.
Its wing spots look like eyes.
The spots scare away birds.

# Green Snake

Look closely. What do you see?
You see a green snake.
It is covered with small, hard plates
called *scales*.
Green scales are hard to see
in green leaves.

# Snail

Look closely. What do you see?
You see a snail.
It lives in wet, dark places.
It looks for plants to eat at night.
Its small shell is hard to see
in a garden.

# LOOK CLOSELY! Hidden Animals
## Comprehension Questions

1. Which animal do you think would be the hardest to spot? Which would be the easiest?

2. These animals use camouflage to protect themselves. Do you think camouflage is a good form of protection?

3. Why does white fur make the polar bear hard to see?

4. What feature of the leafy sea dragon makes it hard to spot?

5. Why do you think the peacock flounder was given its name?

6. What happens to the peacock flounder's skin to help it hide?

7. How does a moth scare away birds?

8. What are scales? Which animal has scales?